A KID'S GUIDE to FISHING SECRETS

by
Dr. Duane R. Lund

Distributed by

Adventure Publications
P.O. Box 269
Cambridge, MN 55008

ISBN 0-934860-37-8

First Printing, 1984
Second Printing, 1986
Third Printing, 1990
Fourth Printing, 1991
Fifth Printing, 1995
Sixth Printing, 1999

Printed in the United States of America
by
Nordell Graphic Communications
Staples, Minnesota 56479

Troy Bates (Staples, MN) tells his neighbor, the author, "My fish could swallow yours in one gulp!"

TABLE OF CONTENTS

CHAPTER I
WHAT MAKES
A GOOD FISHERMAN?

A good fisherman knows about each kind of fish.
- What they eat,
- What time of day they usually feed,
- Where they feed - what kind of bottom or in what kind of weeds, and
- In what depth of water to look for them at different times of the year.

A good fisherman knows tackle.
- How to use different kinds of rods and reels for different kinds of fishing,
- Which live baits work best for which kinds of fish and how to put them to work properly, and
- Which artificial lures work best for which fish and how to best use them.

A good fisherman knows -
- How the weather and the wind effect fishing,
- How to cast right to the exact spot where a fish is likely to be,
- How to jig a lure,
- How to troll and at what depths and what speeds for each kind of fish,
- How to fight a fish and how to land it,
- How to handle a boat and motor safely,
- How to avoid hooking oneself or someone else,
- How to care for fish after they have been caught so they will taste good, and
- How to clean fish.

A good fisherman considers the rights of others who are fishing in the same area.

A good fisherman obeys all laws and catches fish by legal methods only.

CHAPTER II
RODS AND REELS

It is very difficult, if not impossible, to teach someone to cast by having them read a book. Casting is learned through practice. We can, however tell you about the different kinds of rods and reels and give you some tips on how to use them.

SPINNING TACKLE

Spinning rods and reels are perhaps the best all around casting equipment. You can cast most any weight lure and still land most any size fish. The smaller rods and reels, however, are called "ultra-light" and are made for lighter line and lighter lures. Your reel should match your rod: larger reels for heavier, stiffer rods and smaller reels for lighter and more limber rods. Normally, use heavier line with the heavier tackle and lighter test line with lighter tackle.

Open-face spinning reels require rods with larger eyes for the line to pass through. Closed-face reels are used on rods with smaller eyes. Each style rod is made so that the right kind of reel will fit it.

Which is better, closed face or open face? It really doesn't matter. People seem to prefer whichever they learn on or get used to. The open-face does have one advantage: it works better for live bait fishing because the line comes off the reel more easily and the fish is less apt to feel resistance as it runs with the bait. Also, generally speaking, open-face rods are a little longer and more limber, making it possible to feel a light bite more easily.

Both kinds of reels have a "drag" which can be turned to control how hard a fish has to fight to take out line. It is very important to have the drag set just right so that a quick lunge by a large fish will not break the line, yet the runs will make the fish work to take out line, thereby wearing itself out. A properly set drag will keep enough tension on the fish so that it will not have slack line - which would give the fish a chance to throw the hook. Most fish are lost by not keeping a tight line.

When playing a fish always keep the rod tip high; never point your rod at the fish. Let the rod fight the fish. This keeps tension on the fish and a sudden lunge is less likely to break the line.

Two closed-face models.

Open-face reel with matching rod. These rods have larger eyes than rods made for closed-face reels.

BAIT CASTING RODS AND REELS

Bait casting rods and reels have been around a lot longer in our country than spinning tackle. They are fine for trolling or for casting heavier lures, but they are not well suited for light lures and take a little longer to learn to cast well. The touch of your thumb against the spool controls the cast. Release of your thumb starts the cast and you can stop the cast by again applying pressure with your thumb against the spool. A light touch against the spool while the cast is in progress will control both speed and distance. Some reels contain magnets which make possible a smoother cast with fewer backlashes.

Bait casting reel and rod with small, ceramic eyes.

FLY FISHING

The fly rod is so named because it is by far the best tackle for casting flies. It is also ideal for other light lures. Fly rods are used mostly for fishing trout and panfish (sunfish and crappies), but there are times really big fish are in the mood for smaller lures. When that big one hits on a fly rod you will have your hands full, but have confidence in your tackle; a fly rod can whip most any big fish.

Traditional fly casting reel.

Because of the length and flexibility of the rod, fish seem to fight harder and this light tackle can make even the small ones a great deal of fun to catch.

DIFFERENT ROD MATERIALS

Originally, casting rods were made of steel and fly rods of split bamboo. Today, most rods are made of fiberglass. Two relatively new materials, however, have come on the market in recent years. Both are an improvement over fiberglass. They are called "graphite" and "boron." The advantage of these new materials is that they are more sensitive to the bite of a fish; you can more easily feel what is happening on the other end of the line. Both are more expensive than fiberglass, and boron is usually more expensive than graphite. Generally speaking, we get what we pay for, but watch for sales, particularly towards the end of the fishing season.

TIPS FOR CASTING

With all kinds of rods, learn to cast with your wrist rather than your arm. Your casts will be more accurate and it will be far less tiring. Make the tip of your rod do the work. Hold the rod straight up - above your shoulder and along side of your head. Do not cast side-arm.

Practice - practice - practice! In between fishing trips, practice in your backyard. Place an old tire (like a bicycle tire) flat on the ground and try to cast your lure into this target at different distances.

CHAPTER III
LIVE BAIT

MINNOWS

Some people think that minnows are little fish that just haven't grown up yet. Not so. True minnows (like shiners, fatheads, and chubs) just don't grow very big. One exception is the sucker. Minnow-size suckers make excellent bait, but if allowed to grow will eventually weigh several pounds. It is against the law to use other small fish (crappies, walleyes, sunfish, etc.) as bait. As a general rule, no game fish may be used as bait. "Game fish" means any fish on which there are legal limits as to how many one may catch. All others are called "rough fish."

In most cases it is extremely important that the minnows be alive and active on the hook. If you don't have a bite for awhile, check your minnow to be sure it is still active; if not - change it. Some kinds of minnows stay alive better than others. Fatheads and chubs are very tough. Shiner minnows, on the other hand, are quite fragile and will die particularly easily in warm water. During the colder periods of the year, however, shiners stay alive quite well and make excellent bait. During the winter months - especially after the first of the year - fish move more slowly and are less apt to chase an active minnow. That is why some fishermen this time of year clip part of the tail off their minnows so that they will have a difficult time getting away from fish. This also makes the minnow swim a little differently, thereby attracting the fish's attention.

There is an important exception to the live minnow rule. Northern pike and lake trout actually seem to prefer large, dead minnows (like smelt or suckers) in the winter time and early spring. In winter, when using a dead minnow as bait, it is best to use a bobber or a tip-up to keep the bait off the bottom, but in early spring, the dead minnows are best fished lying on the bottom.

When you want to keep the minnow alive on the hook, it is very important not to injure it. The best method is to hook the minnow alongside the back fin (missing the backbone). Point the hook towards the head, because most fish swallow minnows head first and are therefore more likely to get the barb in their mouth. Do not hook the minnow so deeply that it will enter the stomach, and, above all, avoid hitting the backbone.

Insert the hook alongside the backbone with the barb towards the head.

When jigging or trolling with any kind of spinner or lure with which you use a minnow, hook the minnow through both lips with the point up.

When using a minnow on a jig or Lindy hook, pass the barb through both lips, point up.

When bobber fishing with a minnow, give the bobber a little jerk now and then to keep the minnow moving.

It is very important when using minnows as bait to know when to set the hook. If you are trolling with a jig or spinner bait and minnow, set the hook hard, right away, just as soon as you feel the strike. Be careful not to give the fish any slack line or the hook may fall out of the fish's mouth. Keep the rod tip high. There are times when fish seem to bite short and steal the minnow. If this happens several times, try giving the fish a few seconds to get the hook in its mouth, then set the hook.

When fishing with a live minnow on a hook (such as with a bobber), give the fish a chance to get the whole minnow in its mouth as well as at least the barb of the hook. With crappies, you can set the hook after the bobber has been under just a few seconds. With large fish - like walleyes, bass and northerns - give them much longer, at least 20 to 30 seconds. When ice fishing for these larger fish, many fishermen wait until the fish takes out line the second time before setting the hook. Actually when fish are hungry and hitting hard, you can set the hook just as soon as the bobber goes under the water. When fish are not hitting hard, however, it is safer to let the bobber go until it stops, then, when the fish starts to take line the second time, set the hook. Always set the hook while the fish is taking line.

WORMS

Angleworms are favorites for sunfish, perch, and trout. Bunch the worm on the hook so that a fish can not steal it without getting the hook in its mouth. A well-baited hook with plenty of worm catches bigger fish.

The very best bait for sunfish is a fat, juicy **grub worm**. Crappies and even larger fish like them as well.

Nightcrawlers are a favorite walleye bait. Never bunch a nightcrawler on a hook when fishing walleyes. Use a small (#8 or #10) hook and just bury the barb into the "collar" end of the worm, letting it all string out. The danger, of course, is that the fish will miss the hook unless you give it plenty of time to inhale the whole thing. Jigs and other lures may be made more effective by just tipping the hook with a half a worm. This way the fish will be able to smell the lure as well as see it.

The now famous "Lindy Rig" is a favorite way of catching walleyes and bass. Hook the worm as shown:

Bury the barb into the collar end of the worm. The other end is more flat.

Troll the rig slowly, just off bottom. When you feel any tug that you think may be a fish (and you will soon learn to tell fish from weeds or snags), let go of the line immediately. Feed the line out from the reel so that the fish will feel no resistance. The fish will just pull the line through the slip sinker while it lies on the bottom of the lake. After about 20 or 30 seconds, set the hook - hard - and reel in. Minnows and leeches may also be fished the same way on a Lindy Rig or with a split shot for weight (if the water isn't too deep). It doesn't take a fish as long to swallow a minnow or a leech as it does a worm. Use a little larger hook for a minnow (about a #4 or #6).

A bobber may also be used to fish with nightcrawlers. It is best to use a "pencil bobber" or some other thin bobber which the fish can pull under water without feeling it. The smaller the bobber the better. Just hook the crawler in the tip and let it dangle from the hook. When the bobber goes under, let the fish have the bait 20 or 30 seconds or until it makes its second run. If you miss several fish, try letting the fish have it a little longer - up to a full minute.

OTHER LIVE BAITS

Leeches are a very good bait for walleyes and bass. They may be trolled with a Lindy Rig or used with a split shot for a weight. Use a small hook - size #8 or #10.

Leeches may also be used in bobber fishing. Again, the smaller the bobber, the better. Because fish swallow leeches so quickly, you can set the hook a few seconds after the bobber goes under.

There are several different kinds of leeches, but the black "ribbon" leech is best. The dark brown color is also good. Don't use the big spotted leeches you sometimes see swimming by the boat; fish do not eat them.

Frogs are among the best of the natural baits. Small, green frogs are ideal; do not use tree frogs or toads.

Frogs are excellent for fishing walleyes, bass or northerns.

They are best used jigging, trolling, or casting - not still fishing. Frogs may be hooked on jigs or behind spinners, through the lips.

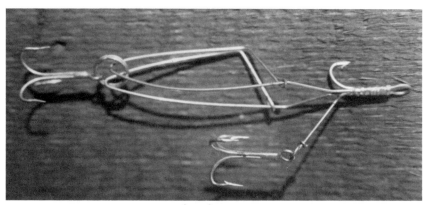

frog harness

A frog harness also works well and helps keep the frog in a natural swimming position.

Salamanders are a good bait for large fish. For some reason, fish don't seem interested in salamanders found on dry land. They seem to prefer those netted in lakes or streams. Ask the bait dealer which kind he has.

Fish salamanders as you would frogs.

When trolling a leech on a Lindy Rig, bury the barb in the larger end of the leech.

When using a leech with a bobber, bury the barb of the hook near the middle of the leech leaving both ends free to wiggle.

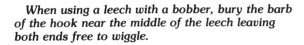

CHAPTER IV
ARTIFICIAL LURES

JIGS

One of the most effective ways of catching fish is to jig for them. The lead weight in the head of each jig makes possible an exciting, natural action as you bounce it along the bottom or just jerk it through the water. The lure itself does not look like any living creature, but the action you gave it can make it very life-like. Try a variety of actions. Some days fish will go for short, sharp jerks. Other times it is better to just twitch the jig every few seconds, and other times it pays to bounce the jig only once or twice a minute, or just "swim" the jig through the water or drag it along the bottom. Experiment!

It helps to bait a jig with a minnow, leech, or piece of worm. Fish can then smell the lure.

Color can also be important. White and yellow are the most popular (especially for walleyes) but bright fluorescent colors are also good, especially in deep or cloudy water. When fishing more than twenty feet deep, white jigs take on a blue tint and yellow turns brown. Sometimes this change of color will affect how well the fish bite.

Many jigs come with hair or feathers. If you tip the jig with live bait, the hair or feathers tend to hide the bait. For this reason, it seems to work better to just use the lead head without any decorations when you are using worms, minnows, frogs, or leeches on the jig. If you do not add live bait, use a jig with feathers like maribou hair rather than animal hair; it has better action.

When jigging, set the hook just as soon as the fish strikes. If the fish seem to be striking short or just nipping off the live bait and missing the hook, tie on a small hook to trail just behind the bait. This is called a "stinger" hook. As mentioned earlier, all you may have to do when fish are not hitting hard is let them suck on it a few seconds before setting the hook. Never use a wire leader with a jig; this will spoil the action. If you are fishing northerns and are concerned about the fish biting over the jig and cutting the line, use a leader made of 20 lb. monofilament line; northerns can rarely cut through it. When fishing walleyes or bass, tie the jig directly to the line; don't even use a snap or swivel.

Use different weight jigs for different kinds of fish. Here is a guide:

kind of fish	weight jig	kind of natural bait used with jig
crappie	1/8 oz.	small minnows
sunfish	1/8 oz. or less	mousies, waxworms, or small grubs
walleyes	1/4 to 3/8 oz.	minnows, leeches, 'crawlers, or frogs
northern pike	3/8 to 1/2 oz.	same as walleyes or with red and white hair or feathers
lake trout	3/8 to 4 oz.*	minnows or small narrow strips of sucker meat
bass	1/4 to 1/2 oz.	worms, minnows, leeches, or frogs

*These heavier jigs are used in very deep water (50 to 100 ft.)

Jigging is an especially fun way of fishing. Fish often hit just as you jerk and the result is a real hard strike. Because the hook is usually caught in the edge of the mouth, the fish will be able to fight to the best of its ability. Remember, however, as mentioned earlier, there are times—such as in cold water in early spring—when fish are more apt to hit a slow moving jig with very little action.

Small spoons, such as Dr. Lund's Little Swede, Swedish Pimples, and Daredevles—may also be jigged with good results. Spoons may be baited by hooking a minnow through the lips (when trolling) or along side the back fin when still fishing or through the ice.

SPOONS, BUCKTAILS, AND BUZZER BAITS

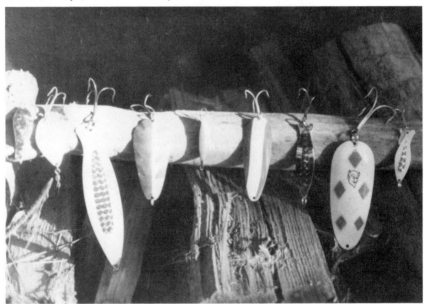

Spoons are among the oldest of artificial lures. They were used by the American Indian long before white man came to the continent. Spoons are probably used more often for northern pike, lake trout, and salmon than any other lures. Smaller spoons are also good for stream trout, walleyes, and even bass. As with jigs, baiting spoons with pieces of worm or minnows may also make them more effective.

Like most artificial baits, spoons are only as good as the action we give them. When casting for northern pike or muskies, use a fast retrieve. When trolling for them, travel at least twice as fast as you would for walleyes. It will surprise you how fast you can troll and still catch northerns or muskies. If your line twists, use a swivel.

Whether trolling or casting, change the speed often. You will find that big fish sometimes hit just as you are increasing the speed.

As stated earlier, small spoons make good jigs, especially when baited.

Color is important, so experiment with different lures if the fish do not bite at first. Some colors work better different times of the year. For example, green is a good color when fish are feeding on frogs. Brown is better when fish are looking for crawfish. Silver spoons are best in spring or fall when shiner minnows are a favorite food because they are found then in shallower water. When the water is not clear or when fishing deep, try fluorescent colors.

Buzzer Baits are quite new as artificial baits go. The spinners set up a vibration in the water which can be both heard and felt by the fish. The spinners also give the appearance of swimming minnows. Buzzer baits work well for northerns, bass, and even walleyes.

Bucktails are an excellent northern or muskie bait. The name comes from the tuft of deer or squirrel hair tied around the hook behind the spinner. They are sometimes hard to cast because they tangle easily, but they troll well.

CRANKBAITS AND OTHER ARTIFICIAL MINNOWS, FROGS, AND CRAWFISH

There are hundreds of these lures which are made to look and swim like natural baits. Although a steady retrieve or speed of trolling may result in good action, it usually helps to change the speed or give the rod tip an occasional jerk. Don't worry about the action being exactly natural. When minnows are thrown into an aquarium with a fish, the fish will usually select the minnow that swims a little differently from the rest. Perhaps this explains why fish hit some really strange looking lures!

Generally speaking, use shallow running lures for bass and northerns and deep running lures for walleyes.

As we will explain later when we talk about different species, how deep you fish is very important. Some fish, like muskies and largemouth bass, will hit baits that swim on or close to the surface. Other fish, like walleyes and smallmouth bass are more likely to hit lures on or near the bottom. You can make a lure run deeper by adding sinkers and/or trailing it farther behind the boat. Some lures run deeper or more shallow with increased speed. Know your lure. Try it where you can see how it responds.

Some lures, such as Lazy Ikes and Flat Fish, can be improved by adding nightcrawlers to one or more of the hooks—but keep the lure balanced by adding to both sides so that the action remains the same. As mentioned earlier, this will not only improve the action but the fish will also be able to smell the bait. You can also improve the action—especially for jigs and spoons—by adding a strip of pork rind.

JERK BAITS

Jerk baits are effective lures for northerns and muskies. Their name comes from the way in which they are fished. The lure itself has little action if you just pull it through the water; you provide the action with sharp, hard jerks of the rod tip while trolling or retrieving a cast. A heavy line and fairly stiff rod are best for jerk baits. Although normally fished near the surface, jerk baits may be used with weights and fished deeper. Even lake trout have been known to hit them quite well.

SURFACE LURES

Plunkers, poppers, crawlers, wounded minnows, and other surface lures are great sport to use for largemouth bass and muskies. They are more effective if allowed to rest a few seconds between jerks. Vary the action.

Surface lures are more effective when used on relatively calm water.

Don't use surface lures if you have a weak heart! The water will literally explode when a fish hits.

ARTIFICIAL WORMS

Plastic worms are especially good for bass. They sometimes work well for walleyes. Try different colors if your first choice isn't productive. Since artificial worms cannot attract fish by their smell, the action you gave them is especially important. How you hook the worm is also important. You may use a worm harness or just bury the tip of the hook in the end of the worm.

A weight ahead of the worm will improve the action. So that you will not jig the worm off the hook, try this method of implanting the hook in the worm:

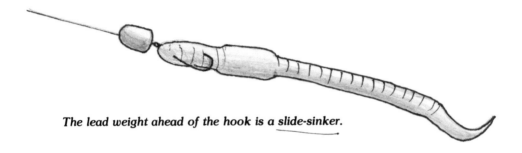

The lead weight ahead of the hook is a slide-sinker.

If the fish are missing the barb, let them have it a few seconds before setting the hook.

CHAPTER V
TIPS ON FIGHTING AND LANDING FISH

The fight begins as you set the hook. It is critical that the hook penetrate the fish's mouth beyond the barb, or the first time the fish has the least bit of slack line, the fight is over and you are the loser! Most larger fish, including bass, walleyes, northerns, lake trout, and muskies, are known for having hard mouths, so set the hook sharply when fishing these species—but not so hard you break the line. Because most lines stretch, the deeper the fish or the farther away it is when it strikes, the harder you must set the hook. It doesn't hurt to set the hook more than once.

Check hooks regularly. Sharp hooks catch more fish because they penetrate the mouth more easily. Carry a small whetstone in your tackle box for this purpose.

Even when fishing the smaller varieties of fish or when using natural bait, it is important to set the hook firmly before starting the fish towards the boat or shore.

As you fight the fish—

- Keep the rod tip high; never point the rod at the fish.

- Be sure the drag on the reel is set properly at the start of the fishing trip. A big fish should be able to strip line even while you are turning the handle; this prevents the line from breaking. Set the drag hard enough, however, so the fish will have to work to take line—otherwise, it will get "slack" and throw the hook. Keep pressure on the fish. Know the test strength of the line; this is your guide for applying pressure or setting the drag.

- Don't "pump" the rod; make the reel pull in the fish. The danger in pumping the rod is that in lifting the tip and then letting it fall back the line goes slack and takes the pressure off the hook. The only exception is in fighting really big fish; just cranking the reel may not apply enough pressure to bring the fish to the net. However, don't drop the rod tip so quickly you create slack line.

- Never reel the fish right up to the rod tip; leave about three or four feet of line between the tip and the fish to give better control. The fish is also far less likely to get slack or break the line.
- When netting a fish, wait until it is well played out.
- Never stretch to net the fish. Let the fisherman bring the fish towards the net; meet him no more than half-way.
- The fish should enter the net head-first. Never chase the fish with the net.
- If the fish is a big one, once it is in the net get it into the boat or on shore immediately. Many a trophy has escaped by breaking through the net or flopping out.

A net is much easier to use than a gaff. However, if all you have is a gaff or if the net is too small, try to hook the fish under the jaw with a quick, hard pull. Lift it into the boat immediately; do not let it flop around.

If you don't have either a net or a gaff, head for shore and beach the fish after it is well played out.

Contrary to what you may have seen on television, **never** put your fingers or thumb into a fish's mouth. Some fish, such as northerns, muskies, or even walleyes, have sharp teeth. Others, such as bass, cannot bite, but a quick flop can throw the hook into your hand.

Even landing a fish with a net has its risks. If you are pulling hard and the hook comes out or the line breaks, the rod or the lure may hit you in the face or eye. Position your head accordingly when landing that big one.

CHAPTER VI
WIND AND WEATHER

Why the weather affects how well fish will feed or if they will feed at all is for the most part a mystery. You and I become hungry regardless of the weather, so why should fish start or stop eating just because the weather changes? Although we cannot say "why," we can tell you some of the effects the weather has on fishing.

One old saying goes:

When the wind is in the east -
'tis neither good for man nor beast;
When the wind is in the north -
the wise fisherman goes not forth;
When the wind is in the south -
it blows the bait into the fish's mouth; but
When the wind is in the west -
'tis then that fishing is the best!

There is considerable fact and logic in this poem. An **east wind** usually means rain or snow or a change of weather in that direction. Stormy weather seems to drive fish into deeper water where they are harder to locate and where they don't seem to feed as well. Not only does a storm mean poor fishing, but it is very dangerous to be on a lake when there is lightning or when it is very windy.

A **north wind** usually means the arrival of what the weatherman calls a "cold front." It means a sudden drop in temperature of 15 or 20 degrees or more. This usually results in poor fishing, but, if you must go out, try deeper water along the edge of drop-offs where changes in weather are less noticeable to the fish. Although a sudden drop in temperature in summer months may spoil the fishing, in early spring or in fall a cold front is not as serious.

Both **south and west winds**, on the other hand, mean stable, comfortable weather. The water becomes more clear and the fish seem to sense less threat from storms in their normal feeding places in shallower waters. South and west winds usually mean good fishing.

Weather has other effects on fish. Immediately following a heavy rain, fishing can be excellent as the run-off washes food into the water and fish sense easy hunting along shorelines or at the mouths of streams. On the other hand, once fish have eaten their fill, they may not feed well again for a day or two.

When stormy winds blow for a day or longer, the lake is stirred-up and underwater visibility becomes poor. As the wind continues to blow, fishing will go from bad to worse. As soon as the weather calms down, however, fishing will improve quickly.

PHASES OF THE MOON

The amount of light the moon reflects at night has an effect on fishing. Even daytime feeders such as the northern pike will feed on a bright, moonlight night. Night feeders, such as the walleye, are inclined to feed more at night during periods of a full or bright moon. If fish hunt food at night, it is logical that they will be less hungry and not hit as well the next day.

We also know that many kinds of fish tend to feed at daybreak or just before dark. As the seasons change, the amount of daylight changes and therefore the time of day when fish have their peak periods of feeding will change.

Such factors are considered in the solunar tables published in many daily newspapers. These predict the best times of the day to go fishing. Since they are based on logic, it does pay to check them if you have a choice of what time of day you will fish. Remember, however, that changes in weather and water conditions can overcome the forecasts of the tables.

FISH & GAME ACTIVITY TABLES™
Computerized © 1983 by Vektor™

Tables indicate beginning fish and game feeding and migration times. Major periods can last up to two hours, minor up to an hour. Adjusted for daylight savings time.

		AM		PM	
		Minor	Major	Minor	Major
Aug.	7	— —	4:52	12:16	7:34
	8	12:50	5:44	12:59	8:07
	9	1:16	6:33	1:40	8:39
	10	1:59	7:25	2:21	9:12
	11	2:50	8:22	3:01	9:42
	12	3:45	9:28	3:40	10:13
	13	4:52	10:57	4:21	10:44
	14	6:09	1140	5:15	11:21

VII
HOW TO FISH
A STRANGE LAKE

Learn all you can the easy way: (1) ask questions of others who know the lake, and (2) watch others who are fishing (being careful, however, not to fish too close; this is considered poor sportsmanship). Beyond that, use what you will learn elsewhere in this book. For example, on the chapter on crappies, we will talk about how in early spring they can be found along the edge of the previous year's bulrushes. In discussing walleyes, we will advise that they may be found along the edge of weed beds, along drop-offs, or on reefs in six to fifteen feet of water.

When fishing a new lake, it is important to locate weed beds. These beds supply shelter and food for the tiny bait fish, and the presence of bait fish means game fish will be there too. Some fish, like bass, can be caught by working a surface lure over the top of the weeds. Others, such as sunfish, may be caught by anchoring and fishing down among the weeds. Still others, like walleyes or northerns, are best fished on the outside edge of weed beds. It is a good idea to mark the edge of the beds for more efficient trolling. The outline of the weed beds can usually be seen on a quiet day when there is no wind; that is a good time to mark them.

Points of land are also good places to look for fish. Points are "key areas" because structure such as drop-offs and weed beds are usually found there. Fish follow these when looking for food.

Bays, too, are a good place to look for fish. This is because bait fish (minnows) often collect there to feed on algae and other tiny organisms. A bay is at its best when a good breeze is blowing towards shore.

Mouths of streams or even small creeks usually mean good fishing. The current carries all kinds of food into the lake and fish often position themselves facing the stream as they wait for "easy pickings."

When fishing rivers and streams, the same rules apply as for lake fishing, but it is most important to look for the deeper holes. Approach these spots carefully so as not to frighten the fish. Let the current carry the bait into the hole—naturally.

Reefs, sunken islands, sandbars, and drop-offs are more easily found with an electronic fish locator or graph. These instruments have the added advantage of actually showing the fish.

A graph-type fish and structure locator.

An electronic dial-type fish and bottom locator.

Once you locate a "hot spot," it will be easier to find next time if you take notes of landmarks on the shore.

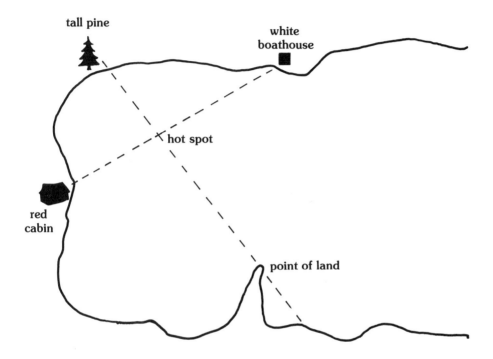

CHAPTER VIII
KEEP A DIARY

There is no better way to accumulate fishing knowledge than to keep a written record of each trip. Fish are creatures of habit and as you look back on a history of successes and failures it will be easy to see certain patterns. For example, if you find you have had excellent luck casting for largemouth bass with surface lures on a late, quiet, June evening along the rushes in a bay of a certain lake after the wind had been blowing into the bay most of the day, there is a very good chance you will repeat that success under similar circumstances. If the pattern holds June after June, you have learned a very significant fishing secret. Be sure, however, you keep a written record; don't trust your memory.

What information should be recorded?

- date
- number, size, varieties of fish
- exact locations
- bait used (what worked and what didn't work)
- time of day (including time of best and slowest action)
- wind (direction and approximate velocity)
- Temperature (especially temperature changes)
- precipitation (rain or snow - heavy or light)
- cloud cover or clear and if it changed whether it made a difference

Successful fishermen recognize the changing feeding habits of fish during each season. Just because we catch walleyes in eight feet of water in a sandy bay in late May does not mean they will be there in mid-summer. A diary will remind you from year to year when it is time to change locations and techniques in each lake or stream.

OFFICIAL
HAYLUNDGA LOG

Date(s) June 2-4, 1983

Captain: Duane R. Lund

Notes

Crew

hot spots! -

Chad Longbella

June 2: Honeymoon Bay

Chris Longbella

6-9 ft. noon - evening.

Kevin Crocker

June 3: Hester's Bay, good

Spike (Mike) Frericks

early A.M. 7ft. poor rest

Pete Franta

of day.

Tom Frericks

June 4: Larson's Reef,

Chuck Moorse

filled out by noon. 10 ft.

Best lures: Lindy Rigs

w/ crawlers. Leeches did

not do much. Caught

Notes

Barometer

some on jigs. Used

30.2 - rising

orange fliver spoons

thru the weekend

around edges of rushes

Weather June 2: cloudy,

for northerns.

10 mph wind from south

90°F, June 3: partly

* fish did not want to

cloudy, slight breeze from

bite when wind was down

the southwest, balmy 90°

on June 3, usually

June 4: cloudy, southwest

found fish along structure

wind, 15 mph, 88°

where wind was blowing in!

To make it easier to keep a written record, prepare a form and make enough copies to last for at least a year. The form reproduced here was designed for use on the author's island on Lake of the Woods, Ontario.

Adding a photo now and then will make your diary more enjoyable

Fishing Log

Total Catch

Date(s)	Walleye	Northern	Bass	Muskie	Other
June 2	32	6	6	0	0
June 3	10	2	1	0	0
June 4	21	7	8	0	0
Total	63	15	15	0	0

Largest Fish

Species	Weight	Fisherman	Catch Location
Walleye	4 lbs. 3 oz.	Kev	Honeymoon Bay
Northern	9 lbs.	Chad	Grassy Narrows
Bass	4 lbs. 1 oz.	Spike	Larson's Reef
Muskie			
Other			
Other			

Hunting Log

Species	Number	Comments

Notes _____

as you study it in years to come. Your written record will be more than informative; it will bring back many good memories. Remember, however, that it is important you record the poor trips as well as the great ones. A good athlete learns as much from failure as success.

CHAPTER IX
SUNFISH

Sunfish are special. Not only are they fun and relatively easy to catch, but they are delightful to eat. If there is ever a public opinion poll taken on favorite freshwater fish for the table, sunfish will probably be #1.

Since sunfish seem to be hungry all the time, the biggest problem is locating them. Fortunately, where we find one we usually find more. Sunfish like to live in schools. Dozens of them, usually of similar size, may be found feeding or traveling together. The exception to this is in late spring and early summer (June) during the spawning season. Sunfish spawn in bowl-shaped nests worked into the sand by their fins. Since these nests are often only a few yards apart, you can still have good fishing once you locate the first one. Sunfish are quite aggressive during nesting time, making them easier to catch. Nesting takes place in relatively shallow water, seldom more than six feet deep and usually less. The rest of the summer, sunfish are found in deeper water in and around weedbeds—usually over a sandy bottom. The depth in which they are found will vary from lake to lake and within each lake during the summer and fall. They can best be located by drifting or trolling *very* slowly. Once you find that first keeper "sunny," anchor the boat so that you don't lose the school. As the water becomes warmer over the summer try fishing deeper. If they are not to be found in weedy areas, try it just outside the weedbed. If that doesn't work, try deeper water yet. In hot weather it is common to find sunfish in depths of 12 to 16 feet, and occasionally in holes over 20 feet. Try fishing a foot or two off bottom and work up from there if you have to. If perch bother, it probably means you are too close to the bottom.

In early spring, just after ice-out, sunfish (and crappies) will be found in very shallow water (one or two feet deep) along rushes or shore weeds from the previous season. They are drawn there by the little creatures they feed on which are looking for warmer water.

Sunfish are usually easy to catch through the ice during the winter months. Since the depth at which they feed will vary from lake to lake and even within one lake, experiment in different areas, starting with the bays. Begin fishing near the bottom and work up if you have to. Depth is very important, so if a friend is catching fish and you are not, measure the distance from the bobber to the bait—exactly.

Now, let's talk bait. Of course, the all time favorite is worms. Either angleworms or nightcrawlers work well but white, fat, juice grub worms are best for the big sunfish. In winter, mousie worms and wax worms (available in most bait shops) are both good—fished either on a bare hook or on a panfish jig or ice fly.

In summer, really big sunnies can be caught on small minnows or miniature artificial lures such as Rapalas, Lazy Ikes, Flat Fish, etc.

Since sunfish have small mouths, it is best to use small hooks (#8 or #10). A long shank hook is easier to remove. If the water is quite clear (especially in winter) use light line—as light as 2# test.

Sunnies are a greedy fish, so when they bite, set the hook almost immediately. If you are using a bobber, and it starts to move across the water, it is time to strike back—you need not wait for the bobber to go under. If the fish are nibbling and not getting the hook, try moving the bait away from the fish in short, sharp little jerks. The greedy sunfish will think the bait is getting away and will probably give you a solid hit.

There are two kinds of sunfish in the Upper Midwest: pumpkinseeds and bluegills. The bluegill is easily identified by the dark blue patch on the gill cover. Pumpkinseeds are more brightly colored and are truly a beautiful fish. The two varieties taste the same and are fished exactly the same way.

CHAPTER X
CRAPPIES

Crappies are a fun fish to catch. When you are into a school of hungry, slab-size crappies—winter or summer—you are in for some real action! Unfortunately, it is usually "feast or famine." Successful crappie fishing, therefore, depends on finding a school. Crappies, like most fish, are creatures of habit, and once you've learned their hangouts, they are much easier to catch.

As a rule, crappies are not fussy eaters, and once you locate them they will bite on a variety of baits—including minnows, small jigs, flies, and grub worms.

We have already said **locating** crappies is most critical to success. When looking for new places to fish them, here are several "rules of thumb" which should be of help:

- In early spring, just after ice-out, look for crappies in the shallows, along old beds of rushes from the previous year or relatively shallow water (four to six feet) just off rocky points. They will be looking for food in the water warmed by the spring sun.

- In summer, work the edges of weed beds. Try trolling, slowly, with a small minnow and spinner or small jig tipped with a small minnow. Once you find a school, still-fishing is effective.

- On summer evenings, try fly fishing for crappies along or over deep-water weedbeds. A little surface popper is a good bait.

- In winter and late fall, fish much deeper; sometimes as deep as thirty to forty feet of water. Schools of crappies will often be suspended—feeding somewhere between the bottom and eight to ten feet below the surface. Try a variety of depths, starting a couple of feet off bottom and working your way up. If crappies have been biting and then stop, you may have to try a different depth or even a different location. If you don't find them, you can always go back to the original hot spot. A power ice auger is a valuable tool for the winter crappie fisherman, because crappies will usually bite once you find them; it is mostly a matter of keeping moving until you do.

When using a bobber, the smaller and more sensitive it is the better. Crappies are delicate feeders and sometimes you can just barely see the bobber move. Usually crappies need only a few seconds to take the bait, so you can usually set the hook right away. Always wait, however, until the bobber is moving or is being held under the water.

Crappies have delicate mouths and you should have a landing net along to keep from losing those big slabs.

Crappies may be either filleted or fried whole (just remove the head, fins, tail, and guts). Crappie (and sunfish) eggs are very good dipped in batter and fried along with your fish.

Some real "slab" crappies, caught by Jon Gerchy, Sauk Rapids. Photo courtesy Jon's father, Ed Gerchy, Editor-publisher Outdoor Outlines, P.O. Box 136, Sauk Rapids, Mn. 56379.

CHAPTER XI
NORTHERN PIKE

Northern pike are the tigers of the northland—the baracuda of fresh water. No fish is more fun to catch—except possibly the musky. Whereas most fish bite because they are hungry, northerns often hit just because they are mean. Northern pike have been known to hit a lure with the tail of their most recent meal still protruding from their mouths. They are a fearless fish, often attempting to swallow adversaries just a little smaller than they are.

Northerns like action. When you cast, vary the speed of your retrieve. Jig wildly. When trolling, change speeds frequently, and travel fast.

Northern pike will hit almost any color, fluorescents and red and white are favorites. However, in spring and early June, when shiner minnows are a favorite food, silver or nickel plated lures are excellent. Because northern often take the entire bait into their mouths, it is wise to use a wire leader.

Sometimes, of course, northerns hit because they are hungry. On these occasions they will even devour dead minnows. Spring lake trout fishermen often have northerns pick their smelt or sucker meat bait off the bottom of the lake. Although large, live minnows make excellent bait for fishing through the ice, dead smelt, ciscoes, or shiners seem to work equally well. When using natural bait, use a 20# monofilament leader. Although northerns are sometimes bottom feeders, it is better to fish a few feet off bottom; they have no trouble looking up. Although northerns hit even natural bait hard, it is well to wait up to a minute before setting the hook so that the fish has ample time to get the hook into its mouth. Some fishermen suggest waiting until the northern stops taking line and then starts the second run. Always set the hook while the fish is taking line.

Troy Bates (Staples, Mn.) with a "baking size" northern pike.

Northerns may be found in a great variety of habitat. Although they are often found along shorelines in the shallows, other times they may be caught in twenty or thirty feet of water and even deeper. Generally speaking, the larger fish of all species are found in deeper water. Indians told early white explorers that deep water northerns were different species of fish and called them "northern pike who live with lake trout."

Weedbeds are a favorite hang-out for northerns. Troll the edge of weedbeds or work lures just over the weeds, just under the surface. A fun and effective way to troll for northerns is with a long bamboo pole. Use your favorite spoon or bucktail and troll at two or three times the speed for walleyes. When a big northern pike hits your fast moving lure it will nearly rip your arms from their sockets!

Be careful when handling northern pike. Their teeth are dangerous and when they throw that big head from side to side they can suddenly throw the hooks of the lure into your hand.

Use a rope stringer; a large northern can easily spring the snap variety.

Northern pike make "good eating," but the bones are a real nuisance. Chapter XVII tells how to eliminate the bones during the cleaning process.

Chris & Chad Longbella, Staples, Mn., display three limits of Red Lake Walleyes.

CHAPTER XII
WALLEYES

Prized for their good eating qualities, walleyes are not known as good fighters. However, walleyes are seldom easy to catch so there is great satisfaction in bringing home a limit.

As with any species of fish, knowing where and when walleyes feed is critical to success.

First, let us talk time of day. Walleyes feed best in the evening, but early morning and mid-day may also be good. If walleyes are not biting well by daylight, chances are they are feeding at night—especially if there is a bright moon.

Walleyes are bottom feeders, but the kind of bottom and depth of water will vary, especially with the time of year. In spring, try sandy bays and places near walleye spawning grounds (streams and rocky shores). They will probably be found in six to ten feet of water. In summer, walleyes move to deeper water. Cold water holds more oxygen and walleyes seem to require more oxygen then most fish. Look for them in ten to thirty feet, usually around such "structure" as weedbeds, drop-offs, sand bars, reefs, etc. Occasionally, walleyes will come up on shallow reefs (four to eight feet) to feed—even on hot days. In autumn, walleyes return to their spring haunts. Not only do walleyes like colder water than most fish, but they also seem to avoid shallow water on bright clear days. One theory is that the sun hurts their over-sized eyes. This may also be the reason walleyes seldom feed on a quiet day when the lake is flat calm. They seem to feed much better if there is some wave action. Fishermen often refer to these small waves as a "walleye chop," because they seem to bite so much better under those conditions than when it is calm. Nevertheless, on cloudy days or in early morning or late afternoon and evening, walleyes do seem to move into shallower water. At night, they may be found as shallow as four feet.

Chad Longbella with a real lunker walleye caught through the ice on Lake of the Woods.

When fishing walleyes through the ice, follow the same depth pattern: ten to twenty feet or more in the daytime and as shallow as four to six feet at night. Some of the best fishing comes an hour or so before sunset up to dark, as the walleyes move into shallower waters to feed.

Because walleyes are bottom feeders, they are rarely caught by casting, unless you can get the bait down close to the bottom. Walleyes will take an enormous variety of artificial and natural baits. Among the most productive are Lindy Rigs (Chapter III) baited with nightcrawlers, leeches, or minnows. Trolling with artificial lures such as Rapalas, Lazy Ikes, Flatfish, etc. is another favorite method. In contrast to fishing northerns and muskies, it is best to troll slowly for walleyes. Jigs are also reliable, especially when tipped with live bait. When fishing slows down late in the summer, try "still-fishing" with bobbers and leeches or night crawlers. In winter, fishing with minnows and bobbers through the ice is the favorite method. Since fish are less active in winter, it is one time you don't want an especially active minnow that will swim away from an approaching fish. One technique is to clip a corner of the tail so that the minnow cannot get away from even a lazy fish.

Sometimes winter walleyes can be coaxed to strike by jigging small spoons (such as the Little Swede) with a minnow hooked alongside the back fin.

As mentioned in earlier chapters, when using live bait, give the walleyes time to inhale it. Set the hook after five to ten seconds when using leeches, ten to twenty seconds for minnows, and twenty to thirty seconds for nightcrawlers. If you miss several strikes, give them a little more time. There are times, on the other hand, when fish are really hungry and you can set the hook immediately.

Perhaps no fish is as drastically effected by a sudden drop in temperature (a cold front) as the walleye. On such days, it sometimes helps to fish deeper, moving very slowly or still-fishing with live bait.

As with all fish, remember to experiment. Don't give up because they do not respond to your first technique the first place you fish. If they don't bite, change lures. If that doesn't work, change locations.

High school All American Swimmer, Curt Jenkins, with Minnesota walleyes.

Jon Edin, Staples, Mn., with a hefty stringer of smallmouths.

CHAPTER XIII
BASS FISHING

Bass are among the most exciting of all fish to catch. Pound for pound they are among the best fighters. Not only are they built like a muscular wrestler, but they dance on the water with the grace of a ballet master, and take to the air like a trapeze artist. Bass fishing is not for anyone who has a weak heart.

Largemouth bass and smallmouth bass are cousins. They look very much alike and fight exactly the same, but in terms of where you find them and how you catch them, they are very different. We shall, therefore, treat them separately.

LARGEMOUTH BASS

The largemouth likes weeds, relatively shallow water much of the time, and is constantly alert to any easy meal that may be on the surface. They have been known to even grab a bird, now and then—perched on a limb just above the water!

Perhaps the most fun way to fish largemouth bass is with a surface lure (such as a Jitterbug, popper, or wounded minnow lure). Cast the "plug" near weeds or water lillies or near a dock or submerged log. As it hits the water, give the lure a little twitch. Bass will often hit at that moment. If not, let it rest 30 seconds, and then give it another twitch or two. Let it rest again, and then continue to work it towards the boat, allowing it to lie at rest occasionally. Bass may strike at any time during the retrieve, right up to the moment you lift the lure from the water. It is hard for the bass to see the lure or its action on a wavy day, so surface lures are most effective when cast into calm water—especially early morning and evening. Night fishing can also be very productive—even without a moon.

Shallow running lures—such as the Bass-Oreno (one of the first artificial lures on the market) are also very effective. Sometimes, however, bass may be found a little deeper, especially in hot weather. Then is the time to try a variety of other lures:

- jigs baited with frogs or minnows,

- artificial worms,

- nightcrawlers on a Lindy Rig or worm harness,

- deep running crank baits or other lures made to represent minnows, frogs, or crawfish, or

- a combination of a bobber with a lively minnow.

Once you have hooked a bass, keep a tight line—especially when your fish leaps out of water and shakes its head.

Largemouths caught in muddy bays may taste a little "strong." If you suspect this may be the case, trim off the stomach meat before frying the fillet.

Bass don't have to be big to be fun. Just ask John Manoukian, Reno, Nevada.

SMALLMOUTH BASS

The smallmouth is more plentiful in lakes along the Canadian border and in the northern parts of the border states. They don't like weeds or muddy bays, but prefer clear water and rocky shorelines. You will often pick up smallmouths while trolling for walleyes—especially if you work into shallow water, close to the shore or a reef. Generally speaking, smallmouths taste better than their largemouth relatives because of the colder, clearer water where they are found.

The smallmouth bass rarely hits a surface lure. It usually feeds right on the bottom. For this reason, jigs, spinner lures, buzzer baits, and deep diving plugs are more effective. Nightcrawlers and leeches are favorite foods and very productive when fished with bobbers or allowed to settle to the bottom—weighed down with a split shot. Minnows, of course, will also work. Because smallmouths are usually found in shallow water, casting small lures towards the shoreline or the edge of reefs can be successful.

Look for smallmouths on reefs, rocky points, and along shorelines where "egg-size" stones are plentiful.

The easiest way to tell a largemouth from a smallmouth bass is **not** by the size of the mouth—both are relatively large (although the large-mouth can open its mouth a little wider). The greatest difference is in the color patterns. The smallmouth is bronze or brownish in color with stripes running up and down. These stripes are more distinct in some lakes than in others. The largemouth is more green and black with a horizontal stripe on each side. Also, the smallmouth has a little red in its eye.

CHAPTER XIV
MUSKELLUNGE

Assorted muskie lures.

Musky fishing is almost a disease! It is only fair to warn you that once you try it, you become addicted for life. Some muskie fishermen want only muskies; they will settle for nothing less. Fortunately for the species, most of these purists release all or nearly all the fish they catch. Once a fisherman has tied into one of these striped acrobats, or even seen the awesome shadow of a lunker following the lure, the fisherman is the one who is hooked!

Some believe there are three varieties of muskies: tiger, leopard and silver. The tiger has spots arrayed like vertical stripes; the leopard has larger spots in no special arrangement, and the silver has faint or no markings at all. Actually, most biologists credit the differences to habitat, interbreeding with northerns, and isolated evolution within one lake. Muskies would probably have disappeared long ago through inter-breeding with the far more numerous northern pike, except that the muskie spawns later in the spring and in deeper water. Even so, some cross-breeding does take place.

Muskies are found in much the same habitat and fished much the same way as northerns. There are some differences, however. Muskies are more inclined to hit surface lures or lures worked just below the sur-face. They are also known to feed earlier in the morning and later in the evening than northerns. Many have even been caught at night, par-ticularly by moonlight.

There is also a difference in the way they fight. Muskies are more in-clined to aerial acrobatics and fighting on the surface. When a musky takes to the air and shakes his majestic head, keep a tight line or he will surely throw the hook.

As with northerns, troll very fast and use an erratic retrieve when casting. Muskies will strike at a slow moving bait, but often miss the hooks or even miss the lure by a foot or more. They are seemingly more intelligent than northerns and behave as though they are toying with a slow moving bait, or are at least suspicious of it. Vary the trolling speed or speed of the retrieve; muskies often hit when you are ac-celerating.

Muskies are found in and along weedbeds, at the mouths of streams, along shorelines, and near or around logs, docks and other underwater structures. Most casting is done into relatively shallow water (3 to 6 feet) or over weedbeds. Trolling is more effective on the deep side of weeds or rushes or along structure (6 to 12 feet deep).

Although musky fishing is associated with over-size lures, many are caught on baits as small as jigs. Bucktails are effective trolling lures while spoons and large jerk baits and crankbaits are fine for trolling or casting. Surface lures, such as wounded minnows, are more ap-propriately used for casting. When using a surface lure, the more com-motion the better. Muskies have a very hard mouth, be sure the hooks are sharp and that the hooks are set **hard**, at least twice.

Both muskies and northerns can sometimes be spurred into action by driving your boat wide open through weedbeds or along the shoreline, then going back and casting the area. More timid fish would flee such a disturbance, but muskies and northerns just seems to get mad.

Be sure to use heavy tackle when hunting muskies. Use at least 17 lb. test line and a leader ahead of the lure.

The fall of the year seems to be the best time to catch the big lunkers, but hot, humid summer days are also productive.

Kevin Crocker, St. Cloud, Mn., proudly displays his first muskie.

CHAPTER XV
LAKE TROUT

Lake trout are a trophy fish. Although limits are small (2 or 3 fish), it is unusual to "fill out." It is a special achievement just to catch a lake trout. Fortunately, they grow very large; one fish can easily feed a family. Although anything over twenty pounds is well worth mounting, the world's record is 103 lbs. (caught in a commercial net).

Because lake trout cannot long survive in water temperatures above 55°F., they are mostly found in deep lakes in the northern part of the United States and in Canada.

In the spring of the year, from ice-out until early June, (later in northern Canada), lake trout may be found in relatively shallow water and are then easier to locate and catch. There are two favorite techniques this time of the year: trolling and bottom fishing from shore.

Favorite trolling lures include spoons, baited jigs, and cowbells with minnows. Try trolling at various depths and at different speeds. Trout often hit just as you speed up. Although must successful spring trolling is near the bottom in 15 to 40 feet of water, trout sometimes lie or feed in "suspension" most anywhere between bottom and the surface.

Spring bottom fishing from shore is a lazy but most pleasant way to spend a day. Favorite baits include smelt, cisco, or a chunk of scaled sucker meat (about 2" by 3"). Use either a fairly large single hook or a #2 treble. A leader made of 20 lb. monofilament line will guard against the fish's teeth and sharp rocks. One or two split shot will help sink the bait to the bottom. Some trout fishermen use a little heavier weight and then insert small pieces of styrofoam into the gills of the dead smelt or cisco to float it off bottom where it will be more visible. Because the trout will probably be feeding in between 10 and 40 feet of water, it is usually too far to cast and it will be necessary to carry the bait out from shore by boat. A depth finder is important in making sure you drop the bait in deep enough water.

Dirk Manoukian, Reno, Nevada, with two hefty lake trout taken from the waters of Great Slave Lake, Northwest Territory.

In summer, lake trout will seek comfort in from 70 to more than 100 feet of water. Although they may be fished with downriggers or steel line, jigging is often easier and more effective. In addition to the traditional lead-headed jigs, artificial lures designed for jigging (such as Sonic and jigging Rapalas) are also effective. The lead-headed jig will usually produce more fish if baited with a minnow or strip of sucker meat. Because of the depth, heavier jigs (2 to 4 ounces) work best. When jigging, start at the bottom and work up. After bouncing or swimming the lure near the bottom, reel it up quickly six to ten feet off bottom. Stop there and jig or swim the lure for a few more minutes. Continue reeling and jigging until you think you are within about 20 feet of the surface. Vary the jigging action; trout sometimes seem to respond better to less action—such as swimming the jig through the water as your boat drifts along the surface. Use the kind of line that stretches least so that you can feel the strike and set the hook more effectively. Because the lure is so deep it may be very difficult to feel a hit. Respond to any tug, no matter how light, with a very hard set of the hook. Setting the hook two or three times at least is a good idea.

Ice fishing for lake trout is slow but often rewarding. Baited jig spoons and airplane jigs seem to work best. Use the same technique just described for summer deep water jigging. Because the water is uniformly cold, trout will again be found in shallower areas. Try 30 to 60 feet of water in the daytime and somewhat shallower in early morning and in the evening.

CHAPTER XVI
STREAM TROUT

Rainbows, browns, and brookies are varieties of trout found in the creeks and streams of the Upper Midwest and Ontario. All of them are great fighters and fun to catch. The rainbow is an able jumper. Trout seem to be among the more intelligent fish and are not easy to fool. If they see you or even feel the vibrations as you walk along the bank, they will not bite.

Fly fishing on the wider, more open streams is considered to be one of the finest fishing experiences. Learning to tie flies that look real enough to fool the fish is in itself a great hobby. There are two basic varieties of flies: wet and dry. Wet flies sink below the surface while dry flies are dressed with an oily substance to keep them afloat. Wet flies are usually designed to imitate minnows or underwater insects, while dry flies represent insects which supposedly have fallen onto the surface of the water and are floating downstream. Success depends on casting to pools where trout are likely to lie in wait for food.

If you do not have a fly rod, spinning tackle will do. To help cast the very light flies, use a transparent, plastic bubble-bobber fastened a couple of feet above the fly. These bobbers may be filled with a little water to make them heavier and easier to cast. Light spinning tackle works well for casting tiny spoons or spinner baits (such as Mepps lures and the Panther Martin spinner).

Narrow, little meadow streams may also be home to some very respectable size trout. Although you may use flies, it is often easier and more productive to use any long rod with tiny minnows, worms, salmon eggs, or even pieces of cheese or marshmallow for bait. Study the stream carefully and learn to know where the deeper holes are located. Be careful so that the trout do not see you or feel the vibration from your footsteps.

Trout need cold water to survive. If the stream temperature climbs above 70° F. for any length of time during the year, they will die.

It may be difficult to use a stringer to keep your trout alive because you are constantly moving from hole to hole. A creel is used to keep the trout fresh. Just stuff it with grass and dip it into the cold stream from time to time.

In early spring, streams that run into the Great Lakes become temporary homes for rainbow trout that spend the rest of the year out in the lake; these fish are called "steelheads." They often grow quite large (over 10 pounds) and are considered to be a real trophy fish, not only because of their size but because they are so difficult to catch. By far the most popular lure is a home-made fly made to look like trout eggs. It is made of several short strands of fluorescent orange yarn, tied to a single hook. In streams where they are legal, trout eggs tied in a little bag made from a nylon stocking and then tied to the hook are also very effective. Both the yarn fly and the trout eggs are best worked along the bottom; you will need split shot to weigh them down.

CHAPTER XVII
TAKING GOOD CARE OF YOUR FISH

FISH YOU RETURN TO THE WATER

If you are not going to keep a fish to eat, unhook it gently (do not squeeze it) and return it to the water carefully. If the fish seems to have trouble swimming, hold it a little behind the gills and move it slowly back and forth in the water. The movement of the water through the gills will help revive it. Each fish we return to the water in good condition means better fishing in the future.

FISH YOU KEEP TO EAT

Fish are a valuable natural resource. Never let them go to waste. Keep fish alive as long as you can, or, better yet, put them in a cooler of crushed ice. If you choose to keep them alive in the water, a fish basket works well—especially for small fish, like crappies and sunfish. A stringer is better for the larger fish, such as walleyes, bass and northern pike. A snap stringer is best for walleyes, and bass, but a northern can easily spring the snap and escape. Use a rope stringer for northerns. With both kinds of stringers, run the point through both the upper and lower jaws so that the fish can open and close its mouth. Never string a fish through the gills.

Run the stringer snap through both the upper and lower jaws of the fish.

Keep your fish out of the sun, in as cool a place as possible. As soon as a fish dies, its eating quality starts to diminish—unless it is placed on ice or kept in very cold water. So clean your fish and put them on ice as soon as you can.

Panfish are usually scaled. However, if they are good size, they may be filleted. If a scaler is not handy, an ordinary spoon works quite well. Next, cut off the head, tail, and fins and clean out the insides. Wash the fish thoroughly.

Larger fish are usually filleted—except really big fish which may be cut into cross-sections—or baked.

Here is a good way to fillet a fish:

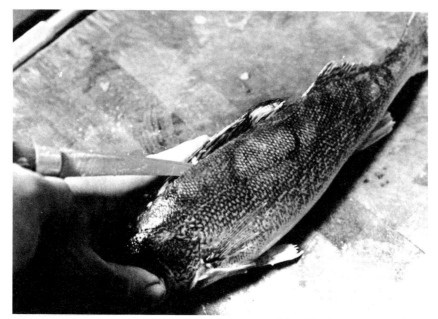

Begin the operation by inserting the point of the blade immediately in back of the head and slightly off center so as to just miss the backbone.

Follow the backbone towards the tail—cutting about halfway through the fish and going all the way through the body after you reach the vent-hole.

Now make a vertical cut along the head, from top to bottom, following close to the gill cover.

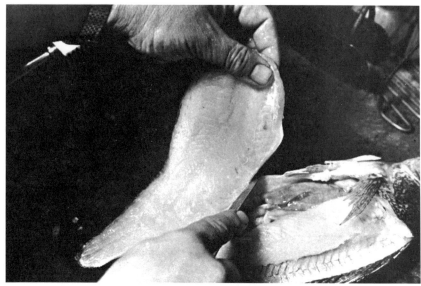

Grasp the loosened fillet at the head-end with your hand that is not holding the knife; as you pull the fillet away from the body, cut with the knife as necessary. Repeat the procedure on the other side of the fish. Now you should have both fillets free from the skeleton.

If you happened to cut through the ribs in the process (some prefer to follow around the ribs), remove the rib cage from the fillet with the tip of your knife.

Remove the skin by laying the fillet on a flat surface flesh side up—and then, starting at the tail end, separate the skin from the meat by sliding the knife flat against the skin and moving towards the head-end of the fillet, holding the tail-end of the skin with your fingers or a pliers and pulling on the skin as you push on the knife. It helps to pull the skin from one side to the other as you move the knife forward. Although the knife blade should be held flat, it will help if the cutting edge is slanted against the skin so as not to lose any meat.

You may want to leave the fillets attached to the tail and then use the tail as a handle in the skinning process.

- If you clean the fish in camp and plan to take them home later, do not wash the fillets, just dry them with a paper towel.
- Bass and northerns from warm or muddy waters may have a strong taste in the belly meat. If you suspect this may be the case, trim away that portion of the fillet.

Northern pike have so many bones, a special method is used to get rid of them:

DEBONING NORTHERN PIKE FILLETS

Northern pike fillets may be deboned (completely). You will have to waste some meat—but it's well worth it. The process works best on fish over three pounds, but with practice you will be able to perform the "surgery" on smaller northerns.

Fillet the northern the same as you would a walleye or any other fish. Leave the skin on the fillet until after you have finished the deboning process.

The ridge of meat containing the bones will be visible. Cut an "inverted V" along the sides of this ridge, but not all the way through the fillet.

Make a horizontal cut between the ends of the "V" at the large end of the fillet.

Lift the ridge of bones in one strip out of the fillet as you release it with your knife.

Run your finger (carefully) down the cut; if you feel any "Y" bones left—remove them. Skin the fillet.

Smaller northerns may be deboned—quickly—by cutting off the tail piece (about 1/4 of the fillet) which usually has few bones. Then make your "V cuts" all the way through the fillet. With this process it is better to remove the skin before you make the cuts just described. You will end up with two rather long, narrow fillets or "fish sticks," plus the tail piece.

If the fillets from a large fish are too thick to fry well (especially if you like your fish crisp), try slicing the fillet in two—lengthwise, with a horizontal cut.

If you prefer to bake a fish, begin by scaling it. Next, cut off the head, tail, and fins. With northerns, the back fin should be removed by cutting about 3/4 of an inch deep along both sides of the fin. It can then be pulled out with a pliers. Cut open the stomach and pull out all of the "insides." Wash the fish thoroughly, being careful to get out all the old blood along the backbone. It is now ready for the oven.

FREEZING FISH

If you plan to keep the fish more than 30 days, freeze the fillets in water to keep them from drying out or suffering freezer burn. Half-gallon milk cartons work well.

If you plan to eat the fish fairly soon, wrap them tightly in freezer paper or foil. If you happen to forget the fish in the freezer for more than 30 days, let them soak in milk while they are thawing.

KEEPING A FISH FOR MOUNTING

Do *not:*

- Clean the fish or even take out the insides.
- Wrap it in paper—especially newspaper.
- Let the fish bounce around in the boat or on shore; they scar easily.
- Put the fish in a live box; they may injure themselves.
- Let the fish spoil.

Things *to do:*

- Wipe off slime (paper towels work well), but keep the fish wet.
- Protect the tail fin by stapling or taping two pieces of cardboard on either side of the tail.
- Smooth down the fins and wrap the fish in a wet dish towel.

- Place it in a plastic bag.
- Freeze. Deliver the fish to the taxidermist frozen.

It also helps to:

- Take a color photo of the fish.
- Wrap the fish in wet moss or grass if ice or a freezer are not available.
- Protect the fish from being bumped while it is in the freezer.

If there is danger of spoiling before you can get the fish on ice—

- Take the entrails (guts) out of the fish through a horizontal cut made along the **side** of the fish below the backbone. **Never** cut open the stomach of a fish you want to mount.

The publisher can't fish but his son knows how! Here's Mark Nordell with a mixed bag of Leech Lake fish—all caught on worms.

CHAPTER XVIII
SIX EASY RECIPES FOR COOKING YOUR OWN FISH

#1 FRIED FILLETS

Wash and dry the fillets (use paper towel).

Make cracker crumbs out of soda crackers. Use a rolling pin. Roll them quite fine so they will stick to the fish better.

Break an egg into a cup of water—in a bowl. Beat the egg until it blends with the water.

Salt and pepper the fillets on both sides.

Cover the bottom of a frying pan with about 1/4 inch of cooking oil and place on the stove over medium heat. All stoves are different, but medium heat or a little hotter than medium is usually about right. If the fish start to burn, you can always turn the heat down.

When the oil is hot, dip the fillets into the egg-water mixture, roll them in the cracker crumbs, and place them in the frying pan. (If the fillets are large, cut them into pieces about five or six inches long.)

When the fillets are well-browned on the bottom side (this usually takes five or six minutes), turn them over. When they are brown on both sides, they should be done. Remove them from the pan and let them drain on paper towels. If you are not sure the fish are done, test a fillet with a fork. It should flake easily and be the same color all the way through.

Serve with lemon or tartar sauce.

Whole panfish, like crappies and sunfish, may be prepared the same way as the fillets, but after they have been browned on one side and have been turned, cover the pan while the fish brown on the second side. Whole fish are thicker than fillets and will cook through more quickly if the pan is covered.

Your fish will never taste better than prepared immediately after you catch them. A shore lunch is a special experience.

#2 POTATO FISH

4 washed fillets
1 egg
2 tablespoons water
1 cup instant mashed potato flakes
1 envelope onion salad dressing mix
cooking oil

Dry the washed fillets with paper towel. If the fillets are large, cut them in two.

Stir together the egg and two tablespoons of water.

Combine the potato flakes and the dry dressing mixture.

Dip the fillets in the egg-water mixture and then roll them in the potato—dressing mix.

Cover the bottom of the frying pan with about 1/4 inch of cooking oil. When the oil is hot, place the fillets in the pan. Brown on each side (5 to 7 minutes depending on the heat).

Drain on paper towel and serve.

#3 FILLETS BAKED IN FOIL

4 fillets
alumafoil
1/8 pound butter
4 onion slices
4 green pepper slices (rings)
salt and pepper

Wash, dry, and salt and pepper each fillet on both sides.

Lay each fillet on a separate sheet of foil.

On each fillet, place a pat of butter, a slice of onion, and a ring of green pepper.

Fold the foil over the fillet and seal.

Place the packages in a pre-heated 300° oven for twenty minutes. Out of doors, the fish may be prepared on a charcoal grill or over a bed of campfire coals.

#4 BAKED NORTHERN WITH RAISIN STUFFING

This recipe works equally well with muskies or whitefish. On the other hand, all fish are not good baked; even the tasty walleye or the flavorful bass are only fair unless they receive special treatment and seasonings.

Northerns or muskies should weigh five pounds or more, whitefish at least three.

Preparing the fish: Scale and gut the fish; remove the head, tail and all fins. Wash and dry the fish, inside and out.

Score the back of the fish with cross-section cuts about three inches apart—down to the backbone.

Salt and pepper, inside and out and in the cuts.

Preparing the stuffing

1 cup raisins
1/4 lb. butter (added to one cup hot water)
2 cups croutons or dry bread crumbs
1 large onion, chopped but not too fine.
salt and pepper
1 cup chopped bologna (or wieners or polish sausage or luncheon meat)

Place the croutons, raisins, meat, and onions in a bowl. Salt and pepper lightly while stirring the ingredients together.

Add and stir in the butter-hot water mixture just before stuffing the fish.

Lay a sheet of foil on the bottom of the roaster.

Stuff the fish (loosely) and place upright on the sheet of foil. Fold the foil up along both sides of the fish—do not cover the back. The foil will hold in the stuffing. If your fish is too long for the roaster, you may cut it in two and bake the two sections side by side.

Leftover stuffing or additional stuffing may be baked in a foil package alongside the fish or even outside the roaster.

Place a strip of bacon and a slice of onion, alternately, over each score (or cut).

Cover the roaster and place in a preheated, 300° oven. After one hour, remove cover and continue to bake until the meat becomes flaky and separates from the backbone (as viewed from the end of the fish). This should take about another half-hour, depending on the size of the fish.

Transfer the baked fish to a platter. Cut through the backbone at each score mark, separating the fish into serving-size portions. The stuffing may be lifted out with each portion as it is served.

Serve with tartar sauce and/or lemon.

#5 POACHED FISH

Fillet the fish, remove the skin, and cut into serving size pieces about six inches long.

Fill a kettle about 2/3 full with cold water. Add 1 teaspoon of salt for every cup of water. Place the pieces of fish into the water.

Add 2 bay leaves, three whole peppercorns, and two tablespoons of vinegar.

Bring to a boil on the stove. When the water is in a "rolling boil" cut the heat back so the water just simmers. Allow the water to simmer about fifteen minutes or until the fish can be flaked with a fork. Do not over-cook; this will make the fish tough.

Remove the poached fish and place on a platter. Flake the fillets with a fork into bite-size pieces. Salt and pepper and brush each piece with melted butter. Or, if you prefer, serve the melted butter in a little bowl by each plate; the pieces of fish may be speared with a fork and dipped in the butter.

#6 FISHBURGER PATTIES
2 cups of flaked fish (take out all bones)
2 eggs
1/4 cup chopped onion
1/4 cup water
1/4 teaspoon salt
1/2 cup bread crumbs or cracker crumbs

Stir all ingredients together. Mold the mixture into hamburger-size patties. Fry on a greased griddle or in a frying pan in a little oil until brown on both sides.

Serve on a hamburger bun spread with tartar sauce.

Teenagers Eric and Greg Peterson of Brainerd, Mn., prove to their uncle, Steve Clabts of Minneapolis, that "kids make better fishermen."

GLOSSARY OF TERMS

Airplane Jig   A jig with metal wings usually fished through the ice for lake trout. The wings make the lure soar through the water when you let it drop.

Bait fish   Minnows or very small fish

Bedding   What worms are kept in

Boron   Material from which some rods are made, usually more expensive than graphite or fiberglass

Chub   A minnow. One variety has a rainbow stripe along its side.

Cold front   A sudden drop in temperature (15 - 20 degrees or more).

Cowbells   A series of very large spinners ahead of the bait; used mostly for lake trout.

Creel   A basket used to carry fish out of water.

Drag   The resistance of a reel to line being pulled out. The drag may be adjusted according to the size of the fish.

Dry fly   Made to float on the surface and imitate insects which may have fallen on the water.

Flat head   A kind of minnow—usually stays alive well. It has little bumps on its nose certain times of the year.

Fillet   A boneless fish steak (one on each side of the fish).

Foil   Aluminum foil—used in cooking.

Gaff   A large hook on a handle—to help land fish.

Game fish   Fish on which there is a legal limit.

Graphite   A kind of material from which some rods are made—usually more expensive than fiberglass and less expensive than boron.

Maribou hair   Feathers from the maribou bird. Because the quill is not used, the part of the feather that is used looks like fine hair. Used to decorate jigs.

Panfish   Sunfish, crappies, and perch.

Pencil bobber   Any long, thin, pencil-shaped bobber.

Plug   An immitation minnow, frog, or crawfish—usually made of plastic. Examples: Lazy Ike, Flatfish, J-Plug.

Poached Fish   Meaning #1: fish taken illegally.
Meaning #2: a way of cooking fish—in a liquid such as water, wine, or milk.

Pound test   A measurement of line strength—10 lb., 20 lb., etc.

Reef   An underwater rocky area surrounded by deep water.

Rough fish   Fish for which there are no legal limits.

School   A group of fish of the same species which travel, feed, and "hang-out" together.

Shiner   A silver-sided minnow.

Sinker   A weight added to "sink" the bait.

Spawning   Laying eggs by the female fish and "milt" on the eggs by the male.

Species   A kind of fish—example: walleye, bass, sunfish.

Still fishing   Fishing from shore or from an anchored boat.

Structure   Sandbars, reefs, logs, weedbeds, etc.

Sunken island   *Not* an island which has sunk! It is a shallow area surrounded on all sides by deeper water.

Swivel   A device which keeps the line from twisting.

Tip-up   A device for fishing through the ice which has a reel underwater so that the line will not freeze in. A little flag goes up when a fish takes line.

Trolling   Pulling a lure through the water behind a boat.

Wet fly   It sinks below the surface; it is made to imitate a minnow or underwater insect.

Other Books by Duane R. Lund

About the Author

- EDUCATOR (RETIRED, SUPERINTENDENT OF SCHOOLS, STAPLES, MINNESOTA);
- HISTORIAN (PAST MEMBER OF EXECUTIVE BOARD, MINNESOTA HISTORICAL SOCIETY); Past Member of BWCA and National Wilderness Trails Advisory Committees;
- TACKLE MANUFACTURER (PRESIDENT, LUND TACKLE CO.);
- WILDLIFE ARTIST, OUTDOORSMAN.
- SENIOR CONSULTANT, THE BLANDIN FOUNDATION.